What you need to know about dates and times in computing

Mike Bain   Ryan Boucher   Ashley Rollke

April 2013

We would like to thank everyone who read a version and provided us with insight.

Gena Kolin, Jess Kirwan, Lauren Crock, Russell Brown, Tim Hordern, Kristan Vingrys, Scott Robinson, Mike Gardiner, Dave Coombes, Dave Reed, Perryn Fowler, Nathan Jones, Mark Lawler, John Magner, Dee Ann Holisky, Pam Malone, Martin Fowler & ThoughtWorks.

Thanks again, Mike, Ryan & Ash.

About the authors

Ryan Boucher

I make going out difficult as I prefer restaurants that have sustainably raised food... otherwise I'll eat the most popular vegetarian dish in Melbourne. Shredded Cabbage! My main interest outside of Thought-Works, is game design; be it board, card or computer. I also like kittens and coffee and whisk(e)y and Jess (mwah!)!

twitter: `@distributedlife`

Ash Rollke

I really like food, rum and boxing, I have found however, that it is not best to enjoy them in that order. I also like testing. A lot. I wasn't always a tester but I'm sure glad I'm one now. I also like Vikings, and rum.

Mike Bain

You should trust what Mike writes because he's been doing stuff for absolutely ages now and is really quite good at it. His achievements include that really clever thing he did once, and this other really hard thing he completed in a tight time scale, thus saving the day. He likes leaning, avoiding the gym and correcting people.

Edited by Gena Kolin

Art and Cartography by us

blog: `http://www.cromulent-testing.com`

twitter: `@CromulentTest`

Read Me!

This book will give you the working knowledge you need to use dates and times in computing. It contains over 30 years of combined expertise and has content on testing, coding, design and user experience. We haven't included many code examples, because once you understand the underlying concepts the programming part is easy.

We'll start by explaining why dates and times are so difficult. Then we'll cover some key concepts and how to deal with user input before taking a look under the hood. We finish by regaling you with some of our past experiences.

To avoid repetition in the testing checklists, we'll assume you will check the following tests without repeating them in every list:

- Happy cases -if it doesn't do what it says on the tin you're in trouble

- Blank cases -leave things blank or filled in with spaces/zeroes

We welcome feedback, bug reports and constructive criticism. Please send it to positive-feedback@cromulent-testing.com.

> **i** These are asides, you don't necessarily need the information in them but we found them too interesting to leave out.

Contents

Part I

Why are dates and times so complicated?

Introduction

One of the reasons that computers will eventually kill us all is they like things to involve simple, logical, repeatable rules. Dates and times, much like humans, are neither simple, logical nor repeatable. In this guide, we'll explain how to test time and how to sidestep a lot of the issues. In this chapter we'll explain why it's a mess, so stay awhile and listen.

One year is defined as the length of time it takes the earth to complete one orbit of the sun. So, to know your position in a year, all you need to know is the earth's position relative to the sun. It sounds fiendishly simple until you actually try and work out the earth's position relative to the sun as you both hurtle around the universe.

One day is defined as the length of time it takes the earth to complete one rotation on its axis. The problem is that the speed of the earth's rotation is in no way related to the time it takes to orbit the sun. This has left us with 365.242199 days in a year, because measuring a year in days is like measuring the speed of a car by watching the steering wheel. So, we've had to add leap years to keep the calendar from drifting out of sync with the seasons. Even if a year was exactly 365 days, it wouldn't help much. 365 is an ugly number that only divides evenly with 1, 5, 73 which makes carving it into regular aligning periods (calendars) problematic.

The Romans gave us sanitation, irrigation and roads, all great things. But Caesar also gave us the Julian calendar, which paid scant regard to digitisation. It counted variable length years and months with weeks. But he made zero effort to align the weeks with anything else, causing the first week in a month or year to often start in the previous one.

In 1582, Pope Gregory XIII introduced the Gregorian calendar, still in use today. He really dropped the ball by ignoring the glaring computational issues, instead focusing on making Easter Sunday easier to predict.

To compound the issues, every man and his dog observed a time of their choosing. This got impractical when rail travel became popular. Try writing a timetable when every stop has a different local time. Time zones simplified things somewhat, but dividing the world into sections is just as political as you might imagine. It created a patchwork of time zones. Despite the fact that at any one time half of the earth is light and the other is dark, there can be 3 days happening simultaneously.

Daylight Saving time makes things more complex. Because of it, locations can change time zones independently whenever they want lighter or darker mornings. This results in tortured computers and broken calendar invites.

If by some miracle you do solve all of the problems and come up with a simple computational calendar, it won't last. Though we treat them like they are fixed, both the earth's orbit and its rotation vary slightly and are gradually slowing down[1].

The reality of our solar system makes dates and times harder than we'd like it. We compound the problem with conflicting definitions and ambiguous language. The latter problem can be addressed by reading on. For the former, you can either read on or move to a metric planet in an orderly solar system.

---

[1]We're all doomed!

When does something begin?

We have many ways to express time, like minutes, months and years. They seem so simple, we scarcely pay them a second thought. However, there are not always 60 seconds in a minute, not all days begin at midnight and the number of days in a month or year depends on which calendar you're using.

When arranging to meet a friend, these ambiguities are an inconvenience. When dealing with computers, this inconvenience is amplified into a problem. When someone says "let's do that tomorrow", they might mean "let's never do this". A computer can only do exactly what you tell it to, regardless of what you may have meant.

When is next Monday?

On Tuesday, 'next Monday' means with some certainty, the Monday in 6 days. However, on Sunday, 'next Monday' definitely means the Monday in 8 days. Between Tuesday and Sunday, 'next Monday' goes through a big bowl of wibbly wobbly timey wimey stuff and flips somewhere in the middle. When it flips depends on who you talk to. Also 'next Monday' and 'this Monday' can sometimes refer to the same day.

What's the first day of the week?

If you answered Monday or Sunday, then you're correct. The Hebrew calendar and traditional Christian calendars start on Sunday, whilst the International Organisation for Standardization has ISO 8601, which starts the week with Monday[1]. Just using the ISO standard isn't enough. Even if you stick to it religiously, your users won't because of their religion.

How long is a day?

You might think a day is 24 hours. But when you consider all possible time zones, it turns out to be 50 hours long. While each time zone will experience only 24 hours, the elapsed time from when the first time zone enters a date to when the last time zone exits is 50 hours.

When does a day start?

Western cultures believe that a day starts at midnight, which we must add, isn't always in the middle of the night. Other cultures believe a day start and ends at sunset. To them we say good night!

What is an afternoon?

What about terms like morning, afternoon and evening? Well, afternoon starts after noon then ends some time before evening; while evening is officially the period between sunset and nightfall. Exactly what period of time these terms cover is a matter of personal experience. You've probably experienced this when you took a half day off to wait for a workman to come round in the morning.

How long is a week?

The Beatles were not only amazing musicians but had a deeper understanding of how different cultures deal with time. It really comes out in their song 'eight days a week'. The majority of the world uses 7 day weeks, but there are cultures using weeks of 4, 5 or 6 days. Dealing with variable length weeks isn't something you'll have to worry about just yet. It's more work, but ultimately don't we want to make software accessible to everyone by using terms natural to them?

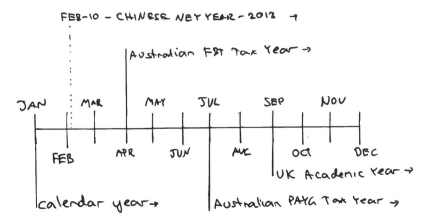

ℹ Going back in history, longer weeks were used by different cultures. The Egyptians used 10 day weeks, 3 week months and 12 month years[2]. The 5 left over days were proclaimed unofficial days, made a holiday and ignored in calculations. Why make all the maths hard because of 5 extra days? They were, after all, only caused by the lunar god Khonsu losing a bet with Thoth[3].

What is a year?

Aside from calendar years (we'll get to those later) there are academic years, financial years and fringe benefit tax years that change from country to country. In Australia, the income tax financial year starts on the 1st of July, and the fringe benefit tax financial year starts on the 1st of April. The calendar year starts on the 1st of January.

The Chinese New Year is based on a lunar calendar and therefore has a different length, so its date moves around on the Gregorian calendar.

As we can see, these types of years can start at different times and run for different lengths.

FEB-10 - CHINESE NEW YEAR - 2013 →

Australian FBT Tax Year →

JAN · MAR   MAY   JUL   SEP   NOV

FEB   APR   JUN   AUG   OCT   DEC

UK Academic Year →

calendar year→   Australian PAYG Tax Year →

There are different ways of measuring a year, other than using a calendar.

- Lunar year -the time it takes for 12 full cycles of the moon
- Solar or Tropical year -the time between certain tilts of the earth relative to the sun
- Anomalistic year -the time between earth being closest to the sun in its elliptical orbit
- Sidereal year -the time it takes the earth to complete one orbit of the sun based on a fixed point like a star

Part II

Key concepts

What is a point in time?

You need to make sure that your time is both precise and accurate, otherwise you're leaving an opportunity for bugs. Take Tuesday 27th of March, like all points in time it will have the following attributes; precision, accuracy, relevance and range. The differences are subtle but it's important not to misinterpret the information.

Precision - The unit, be it minutes or millennia, you choose when you specify the time, defines its precision. The smaller the unit, the more precise the time point is.

Accuracy - How close is it to the true time? This is different to precision, a wrist-watch may have second-level precision but be inaccurate because it's an hour slow. In this case, increasing the precision won't make the watch any more accurate.

Relevance - How useful is the time to the person using it? Nanosecond precision is necessary in the internals of a computer but an annoyance if you just want to know how long it is till lunch. Increasing precision does not necessarily increase relevance.

Range - Planck time is the smallest theoretical unit of time[4]. If you use any other unit, you're actually stating a range encompassing all the smaller units. The time 9:15 am, includes all seconds from 9:15:00 to 9:15:59.

While we are on the topic of ranges, a time range can be bounded or unbounded. The Precambrian Period ranges from about 4,600 to 543 million years ago. It's a bounded range meaning it has both a start and an end. The uptime of the computer, upon which we write, is 100 days, is an ever increasing unbounded range.

A point in time can refer to a fixed point in the past, present or future. It can be relevant, precise and accurate. It can be a range bounded or unbounded or a single point in time.

Time zones

People used to observe a local time based on whatever took their fancy. This worked just fine until the invention of railways. Each town added to the railway network could have a local time out of whack with the others. As you might imagine, this made timetabling increasingly nonsensical.

In 1840, to address the confusion, the Great Western Railway introduced Railway Time. For the purpose of train travel, the United Kingdom would use the time set by the Royal Observatory in Greenwich. Although unpopular at first, Greenwich Mean Time (GMT) soon became the standard and was enshrined into law in 1880[5].

The idea behind time zones is practical. Rather than letting every village choose its local time, the world is divided and you adhere to the time in your zone. This gives each region a local time approximate to the local solar time and the world gets an understandable global time reference.

Time zones are named, and when written, they are often abbreviated. For example Melbourne, Australia uses EST. EST refers to "Eastern Standard Time" in both Australia and North America. It also refers to "European Summer Time". So be careful saying your offer closes at 5 pm EST.

Time zones are written as an offset from UTC (we'll explain UTC soon). For example, Melbourne's normal time zone is UTC+10 meaning it is 10 hours ahead of UTC.

Because of the way time zones overlap, there are sometimes periods when 3 dates are happening at once.

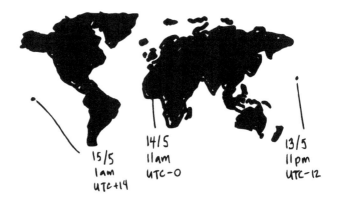

Anchoring

Unanchored time is deliberately without a time zone. If my alarm is set for 7:30 am, then regardless of what time zone I am in, my alarm will go off at 7:30 am. If I have a meeting at 12:50 pm (Melbourne time), this time is anchored to Melbourne time[6]. If I fly to Perth (3 hours behind Melbourne), I need to know that the meeting will be at 9:50 am (Perth time).

Be careful which one you chose, if you store the time unanchored (without the time zone) and at some later point you need to convert the time to a different time zone, you're left with two options.

1. Cross your fingers, assume the time is correct and leave it as it is.

2. Guess the original time zone and then convert it to the new one.

If you have multiple times in different time zones, for example a flight that's taking off in one time zone and landing in another, it's almost impossible to convert one without breaking the other. For example:

- Flight Departs: 7 am Melbourne time
- Flight Arrives: 7 am Perth time

As we've not stored the time zone, we really have only this information:

- Flight Departs: 7 am
- Flight Arrives: 7 am

Now, what time will it be in Melbourne when your flight arrives? As you can see storing the time zone is worth the initial effort.

Time Zone Oddities

Despite the good intentions of time zones, people have gotten involved and all sorts of peculiarities have cropped up. Here are some situations to be cognisant of.

Time zones can change

In 2011, Samoa wanted to change from the last time zone to the first in order to better align with their trading partners. They did this by hopping the International Date Line and skipping December 30th that year. American Samoa, an unincorporated territory of the United States, is adjacent to Samoa. As American Samoa has very close ties to the US, it did not change time zones. There is now a 24 hour difference from one end of the islands to the other.

American Samoa UTC −11

Samoa UTC +13

Unofficial time zones

In Australia, on the border of Western Australia and South Australia, there is a time zone, Central Western Time, that's just 15 minutes off South Australia Time. It's unofficial in the sense that it's not government mandated, but the locals adhere to it. There are five places in Australia that use it exclusively[7].

Officially following nearby timezones

Some towns that sit on a time zone border follow the neighbouring time zone rather than the official one. Broken Hill, in New South Wales, Australia, is classified as EST but follows the time zone of South Australia, which is Central Standard Time. The time difference between them is only 30 minutes, but due to the width of the state it'll be dark on the east coast and still light in Broken Hill[8].

Time zones and month or year boundaries

Obviously people reside in different time zones. If you're planning with a friend to do something next month/year, you need to make sure what that means in their time. If it is December for your friend, they will think next month is January. You might already be in January, so next month for you is February. Remember that two, sometimes three dates will be occurring at the same time.

Nested Time Zones

Within the United States of America (follows DST) lies Arizona (no DST) and within Arizona is the Navajo Nation reserve (follows DST) which within itself contains the Hopi reservation (no DST) which within itself contains a small Navajo Nation chunk (once again follows DST)[9].

Tips:

- Unless you know you want unanchored time, always store the time zone with the time, you'll need it later.

- Be aware of unofficial time zones when localising.

- If you don't display the time zone, the user will assume it's their local time.

- Does it make sense to let people specify the time zone?

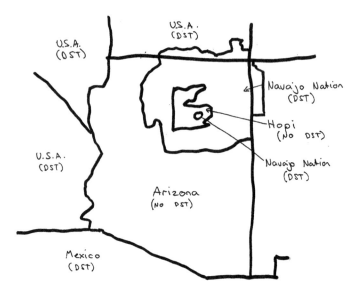

Nested time zones in the United States.

Tests:

- Does the UI show the time zone?
- Try time zones with 15, 30 or 45 minute offsets
- What happens when a user takes a trip and changes time zones?
- What happens when a country changes time zones?

Daylight saving time

Are you always running out of candles? In 1784, Benjamin Franklin proposed an idea to save them called Daylight Saving Time (DST). The idea was simple, move the clocks an hour forward in the summer. You'll get more daylight in the evening and burn fewer candles. All you had to do was re-orient your sundial twice annually. It's debatable if this saves energy in the modern world[10].

When we say we put the clocks forward or back, what actually happens is your location switches to another time zone. For example, in the UK, the standard time zone is Greenwich Mean Time (GMT); for the summer, it changes zones to British Summer Time (BST).

Different regions change in and out of DST independently and some even vary the date of switch from year to year. This means the time difference between two regions can vary. As all of these shifts in time zones are non computable, they need to be looked up whenever you use time. The IANA currently maintains the Time Zone database.

Are we still meeting at 10?

You have a phone call with a friend in a different country at 9:00 am. For them, it's at 10:00 am. Before the call, you shift out of daylight savings time. Now, 9:00 am for you is 11:00 am for your friend. Does the meeting stay at 9:00 am your time and move an hour for your friend or move to 10:00 am your time so it stays the same for your friend?

Are we skipping things?

To go into DST, the noticable effect is that the clocks go forward one hour and jump from 2:00 am to 3:00 am, what happens to your batch job that was supposed to run at 2:30 am?

Are we doing twice as much work?

To come out of DST, the clocks effectively jump back one hour at 3:00 am, this can cause havoc with log files as 2:00 - 3:00 am happens twice. How do you sort log entries when the same hour happens two times in a day? If you have a system that calculates the average over the past hour, will it still work during the switch.

The truth is out there.

Have you noticed that we're asking a lot of questions about Daylight Savings without providing any answers? We're not going to leave you in the dark. An answer exists for your DST woes; it's called UTC. This three letter initialism will brighten up your day more than a little daylight ever could.

Tips

- Don't use local timezones; read the next chapter.

Tests

- Run your overnight jobs during the daylight saving switch.

- What happens if you have multiple time zones and just one of them goes into DST?

- Set the time to be just a before a DST switch. What happens to your transactions and logs?

- Store a date, what happens to it going into and out of DST?
- Try a transaction that bridges a DST switch.

UTC

As we've shown, there are many confusing elements to storing dates and times. UTC is the international standard designed to, avoid the confusing elements. It's free from the blight of DST and almost perfectly suited for what you need.

UTC stands for Coordinated Universal Time, obviously. The English wanted it to be CUT for Coordinated Universal Time and the French wanted it to be TUC for Temps Universel Coordonné. Given the checkered history between the two countries, the initialism UTC was chosen as a compromise to stop a repeat of the 100 years war.[2]

UTC is a coordinated time; that means it's manually adjusted to stay within 0.9 of a second of Universal Time 1. UT1 is the time defined by the earth's rotation. For most intents and purposes it's as accurate as you will need it to be.

UTC is time measured from earth and generally for earth. If you were not on earth you would not be able to determine the time the same way and without synchronising at regular intervals your time would drift. The International Space Station (ISS) uses UTC+Z.

---

[2]How do you please everyone? By pleasing no one.

i Ironically, in this universe there are multiple universal times. Each has a different way of calculating the time whilst dealing with the earth's irregular orbit[11].

- UT0 - Calculated from the motion of stars or extragalactic radio sources and laser ranging the Moon and satellites. UT0 doesn't handle polar motion.

- UT1 - The best we've got, it's calculated from observations of distant quasars and laser-ranging of the Moon and satellites.

- UT1R, UT2R - Smoothed versions of UT1 that filter out variations caused by things such as tides, atmospheric weather or plate tectonics.

- UTC - Kept to within 0.9 seconds of UT1

UTC and time zones

UTC on its own isn't actually a time zone, it's a reference for other time zones to define themselves. For example, Melbourne is UTC+10 whilst Beijing is UTC+8. The time zone that represents the time in UTC is named UTC+0 or UTC+Z.

If all servers are storing their dates in UTC+Z then it's simple to communicate with each other, as no conversion needs to occur. We also don't need to worry about DST as UTC+Z doesn't have daylight saving time.

Leap seconds

While UTC simplifies using and storing time, it has one thing that can bite you in the arse. Every 18 months or so, a leap second is added to keep it close to UT1. This is important to remember as you'll experience minutes with 61 seconds. This causes problems every time it happens. The most recent, in June 2012 claimed many victims including the Network Time Protocol (NTP), BuzzFeed, Foursquare, Yelp, LinkedIn, Gawker, and StumbleUpon[12, 13].

To work out the number of seconds between two dates in the past, one needs to look up when/if leap seconds have occurred. Leap seconds are difficult to predict they're only announced 6 months in advance. Therefore, it's not possible to accurately count the number of seconds between two dates outside this margin.

In 2015 at the World Radio Conference a decision to abolish leap seconds from UTC may be made.

The basic rule of UTC is: if you're not sure if you need to use it, then you need to use it.

UTC is for storing time in computers. Before showing the time to a person, convert it to the user's current time zone; which may be in daylight saving time. Remember, some DST may apply once you leave the safety of UTC.

> **i** GPS systems don't include the leap seconds so they're drifting away from UTC[14].
>
> Google doesn't strictly use UTC either. They deal with leap seconds with a cool technique called Leap smear. They modified their internal NTP servers to gradually add a couple of milliseconds to every update, adding the extra second over a time window before the leap second actually happens[15].

Calendars

There are many different types of calendars although, when using a computer, you're generally stuck with the Gregorian one. Other calendars are not well represented because of the Gregorian's prevalence in Western society. For you, this means that apart from working out when a few holidays occur, you can mostly ignore all the other calendars. Hopefully this will change in the future. It's more work for us, but computers should be doing the work, not the people using them.

Lunar calendars were common in the past; they measure the time between lunar phases. The Lunar calendar's early popularity was possibly because the cycles of the moon are much easier to track than the cycle of the earth's orbit of the sun.

For example: "Is the moon full?" or "Are we in an equinox?"

One required looking at the sky, the other a thousand of years of civilisation.

A lot of holidays and festivals, like Easter, are based on a Lunar calendar. This causes the dates of these events to change from year to year when represented on the Gregorian calendar. Easter Sunday is defined as the first Sunday after the full moon following the northern hemisphere's March (or Vernal) equinox. That's why Easter Sunday can be anytime between March 22 and April 25.

Some calendars, like the Islamic calendar, still follow the Lunar cycle. It is used to calculate the dates for Ramadan and Eid, among others. Its years are 354 or 355 days long so it drifts relative to the Gregorian calendar, the solar year and the seasons by 10 or 11 days each year. Once every 33 years it synchronises with the seasons.

As you'll see, the relationship between computers and calendars is quite small, so it doesn't really matter if the calendar used doesn't match a solar year.

Calendars and computers

Computers have their own calendars based on things like the number of seconds since 01/01/1970. They're great for storing as all you have is an integer but you have to convert it before showing it to a person.

A weekend is fairly easy to determine and there are many libraries out there that do it for you. A public holiday is harder as governments don't announce the dates very far in advance. Public holidays come and go and some only occur in certain regions. To check for public holidays into the past, you will need the calendar for that year and that region.

If you were writing a billing system and the due date landed on a weekend, then you would need to alter it. Usually, it's moved forward to the next business day. It gets tricky if it's a public holiday which isn't considered a business day either. Every year, for all the countries you have customers in, you'll have to add a calendar containing the public holidays.

The next level of complexity is collaborating with international partners on what is a day where you're all going to work as you may not share a common working week. It's common in the middle-east for a Friday-Saturday weekend and in the past it was a Thursday-Friday weekend[17].

---

i In case all of this is too simple for you New South Wales has the first Monday in August as a holiday for bank employees only[18].

Julian Day Number

If all you care about is days, then the Julian Day Number is for you. It counts the days, as whole numbers, since the 1st of January 4713 BC[19]. As this method only uses days, all the trickiness associated with variable length months, years and calendars goes away. When we wrote this the Julian Day was 2,456,387. The following day was 2,456,388 and so on.

The Julian Day Number is most useful if you're counting days. If you want bigger or smaller units then you have the added complexity of conversion, making it easier to stick to UTC.

Don't cross the streams, you can't bring in Gregorian calendar concepts to Julian Days. If you add 365 days to a Julian Day to get the date next year you're going to have a bad time.

Leap years

Hacking existed long before the computer age. Take this classic example:

A Solar (or Tropical) year is a little under 365.25 days. The Gregorian calendar is 365 days.

When a year is divisible by four, we add an extra day to stop the calendar from drifting out of sync with the seasons. However, as a year is a little under 365.25 this over-corrects the drift[3]. To fix this, if the year is divisible by 100, we don't add an extra day. This under-corrects the over-correction correction so to fix that, if the year is divisible by 400 then we add the day. Clear? After all this, the Gregorian calendar still drifts off by about 1 day every 8000 years. Close enough.

So, a leap year is a year that is divisible by 4, that is not divisible by 100 unless its also divisible by 400.

The extra day, in the Gregorian calendar is February 29th. It occurs just infrequently enough to take programmers by surprise. Leap year bugs have claimed many companies, recently including... well we don't want to be too libellous in our first book, so do a Google search for "leap year bug" and you'll see what we mean.

Tips:

Use a trusted date-time library

---

[3]Drift is only OK if you're a tofu delivery boy

Tests:

- Start on a leap day

- Contains one or more leap days (is the duration calculated correctly?)

- End on a leap day

- Anniversaries (Feb 29, 2008 -> Feb 28, 2009)

- Try valid leap days (Feb 29, 2000)

- Invalid years (Feb 29, 1900; Feb 29 2001)

- Run batch jobs that start or finish on a leap day

Part III

Dealing with user input

Getting a date from a user

So dates and times are confusing, ambiguous and commonly misunderstood. In this part we look at how to collect them from users. We'll cover some questions you should ask yourself before you start, and we will provide guidance on common date and time controls.

Why do so many websites ask for your date of birth? Have any of them ever sent you a birthday card?

Do you need a date?

We can make using dates and times simpler by not using them at all.

Some websites ask for the user's age to determine if they are old enough to view the content. Because no one has ever lied on the internet, this foolproof method has made it a child-friendly wonderland. Making the user do more than is necessary, coupled with privacy concerns, results in a poor user experience.

As online age verification is dubious, unless you have a legal requirement, you may as well make it convenient and easy to test. A good example is when you create a Facebook account you have to check the, "I agree that I am over 13 years old" checkbox.

What culture are your users?

When you have the following date 01/05/12 it means the 1st May 2012 in most of the world, 12th May 2001 in China or Japan and the 5th January 2012 in the USA.

Most of the world writes the date with the day first, dd/mm/yy. The Chinese and Japanese tend organise things largest to smallest, so they write yy/mm/dd. They also do this with addresses. North America trolls the rest of the world with mm/dd/yy and the imperial system. Canadians, not wanting to offend, use all three formats.

You can reduce the confusion by using non-numeric months. Instead of 11, show November.

The worst example of formatting a date we could find comes from the Oracle BRM system with mmddhhmmccyy.ss[20]. That's right: months, days, hours, minutes, century, year, decimal point, seconds.

ⓘ Some countries use Roman Numerals on their postmarks to represent the month. So a date of 05-V-2012 is the 5th of May.

Are you going to show a default date?

If you know roughly what date you're expecting, you can set it as the default. It's more efficient for people to adjust a date when needed than to enter one from scratch every time. Although, you do run the risk that the user may just stick with a potentially incorrect default, or not even notice the date at all.

Are your dates inclusive or exclusive?

Most of the time people use inclusive dates. When you search for a flight between two dates, say March 1 and March 15, you expect both of those dates to be included.

Exclusive dates are when one or both dates are not used in the range. While less common than inclusive dates, it still occurs. As always, tell people what you want. A billing system we worked on once would date invoices March 1 to April 1. March 1st was included in the billing cycle but April 1 was not. This caused customer enquiries.

Things to test for all date entry fields

- Today
- Tomorrow
- Yesterday
- Invalid dates 29/02/(non leap year), 31/04/2012, 1/13/2012
- Select the fields out of order
- Old dates, the oldest you would expect and a historical one like 1066
- Future dates, to infinity and beyond
- Play with the time on your test machine
- Skip the client side validation, ensure the server can handle the funk

- Edit the date after submitting it

Things to test for all date ranges

- Start and end date are the same

- End date before the start date

- Make the start/end/both dates invalid

- Make ranges as big/small as possible

- Range entirely in the past/future

- Start in the past and end in the future

- Cross a week/month/year boundary

Visual Calendars

This is great method for selecting dates in the near future and the recent past. It can save a lot of work on client side input validation. However, for dates further away, users will have a lot of clicking to do as they cycle through each month.

Tips

- Indicate visually the dates people can't select

- Default to appropriate range

- Remember their selection, even if they navigate away

Tests

- Change to last/next month

- Change to last/next year

- Select a date then scroll to a different month/year

- Pick a date on the calendar, then type something else in the field

A Trifecta of Drop Downs

This date picker works well for dates within a few decades. Like below, you can use the name of the month, instead of the number, to avoid ambiguity. The drop down options handle most of the input validation, although you will still have to check for invalid dates e.g. April 31 and leap years: Feb 29, 2012.

A potential downside is, if you wanted a date of birth, the oldest person is currently 115 with 122 being the oldest verifiable age. As most sites are for over 13s you're left with a likely range of 102 years, that's a pretty big drop down.

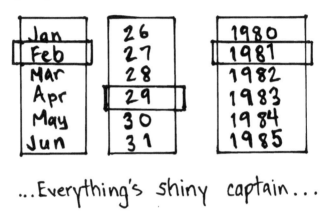

...Everything's shiny captain...

Tips

- Re-verify the date whenever the month or year is changed because it's easy to select invalid dates, e.g. February 31

Tests

- February 29 leap year/non leap year

- April/June/September/November 31

- Type in the fields after selecting them

Plain text field with visual dividers

The field is pre-populated with little dividers that show where each of the date parts is meant to go. This can be a lot faster than selecting dates from pickers or drop downs, especially for dates far in the past or future. All the validation will be up to you.

Due Date [9 / 5 /2012]

Tips

- Show what format you want: 'dd/mm/yyyy'
- Limit the field lengths
- Only allow numbers

Tests

- 1 digit 1/1/1
- 2 digits 01/01/01
- 2 and 4 digits years
- Mix it up 1/02/2012
- Invalid dates 29/02/2011, 31/04/2012, 1/13/2011
- Delete the separators, replace them with something else
- Insert symbols ' " \ / \/ * % ^ & # $ -) !
- Letters 1O/1b/2er5
- Enter them backwards

Plain text field

A plain text field lets the user type whatever they want, and they will. All the validation is up to the server and by this we mean you.

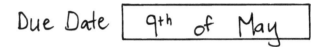

One advantage of this control could be to allow people to freeform and type in values like 'next monday'. But, natural language processing is hard and beyond the scope of this book.

Tips

- Don't use plain text fields, they're a lot of work.

- Tell people what format you expect, 'dd/mm/yyyy'

- Be very strict with what input you accept

- Limit the field length to the expected format.

- Echo back what you've determined their input means

Tests

- All of them!

ℹ️ Sometimes for fun, Ryan puts in a date in with a capital 'O' which looks like an 0 and then raises a bug report. Like so: 3/3/2O12.

Getting the time from a user

Do we need the time Mr. Wolf?

Until the invention of time, no-one was ever late. Sadly, this laissez-faire existence ended when the Egyptians invented shadow clocks. Nowadays, in modern times, there are two main ways to represent time. The majority of the world uses the 24 hour clock. The USA, Canada and Australia mostly rely on the 12 hour clock[4] annotated with am (ante meridiem) and pm (post meridiem).

---

[4]Why didn't anyone tell us?

Seize the day

Never feed gremlins after midnight. Late night users can get confused about which day they're in. People tend to organise around their sleep cycle. When out for the evening, 01:00 feels like the day you went out, instead of the morning after. A Melbourne daily travel pass takes this into account and is valid until 03:00 the next day.

Imagine it's late, you're tired and you set your alarm for tomorrow morning as a one-off. When you hit save, it says "Alarm set for 8 hours from now." Feedback in this format is crucial. Had it said "Alarm set for 9 am on the 13th" you would be asking yourself is the 13th today or tomorrow? Had it said "Alarm set for 9 am tomorrow" you might have worried what day your phone thought 'tomorrow' was.

On any longer time scale, the displaying of the number of hours would be terrible. Who needs a message saying "Your dentist appointment will be in 257 hours"?

Make use of absolute dates

Showing a relative date like "next Friday", to a user leaves an opportunity for misinterpretation. As we've already discussed, terms like "next _____" can be confusing. Show them "next Friday", is "Friday the 13th", so they can avoid Camp Crystal Lake.

50

Complicated Domains

The ATO (Australian Tax Office) requires a Business Activity Statement to be submitted four times a year. To the ATO, quarter 3 (Q3) covers January 1st to March 31st. This period of time is considered Quarter 1 by non accountants. Even if you're an accountant, it's confusing.

So, if you're making a taxation application, especially one designed for people who are not accountants, consider calling out the date range for Q3 whenever possible. Adding strict validation around the date inputs, with helpful messages, will improve things. But, there's only so much you can do with large fonts. Ultimately, the answer might be to simplify the problem by simplifying the domain.

Never trust the client's time

You should never trust the client's time. Their time may be wrong or from a different time zone. Dishonest users often exploit applications by changing their client's local time. We repeat, never trust the client's time.[5]

Even honest computers won't provide you with consistent or accurate time. Computers, like any clock, can lose time or run fast. To work around this, you can sync your computer's clock with a time server. This is good enough for most things, but not tasks that need very high accuracy or precision. This infrequent syncing results in a clock that's a few milliseconds out most of the time.

Decimal time

One of the crimes that many timesheet systems commit is to use decimal time. It might make perfect sense for accountants billing in 6 minute increments, but for the rest of the universe, avoid this if possible. No one enjoys entering .67 of an hour instead of 40 mins.

---

[5]That's a big 10-4

Choosing a time control

- Consider what you want, before you choose a time control.

- What are you using the time for?

- How precise does the time need to be?

- Do they need to select am/pm or is 24-hour time preferred?

- Do they need specific time or will fixed intervals do?

Tests

Here are some common tests that should be run against whichever time control you choose.

- Are you using 12 or 24 hour time?

- How obvious is the am/pm part?

- Select 00:00:00 -then go backwards

- Select 23:59:59 -then go forwards

- Select times in the future/past

- The 60th second, remember leap seconds

- A range crossing day, month or year boundary

- Different time divisors 23:00, 23.00, 23h0

- Change the system clock to be before/after the server

- What happens if a user is in a different time zone?

Let he who hath never booketh a meeting at 5 am cast the first invite.

Time Spinner

A spinner allows the user to click up and down to change the value by one; a click-and-hold spins the time faster. On a handheld device this control allows for flick spins. A third option is to click in the middle and type in the time.

The speed of the long click is hard to get right and may be frustrating for the user.

Most phone applications use a combo spinner input field that supports only two numbers. Increment and decrement works well for 5 minutes from now while typing is faster for longer time jumps. These do the job on a touch device because the keyboard and mouse are together in one. On a webpage it's cumbersome to go from clicking to typing.

Time drop downs

One setup is to have a drop down for the hour, minute, second component. It's a bit awkward and hours may go to 24 or you may have a radio control for am and pm. The minutes become painful as you have 1 of 60 to select.

This can be condensed to one single drop down with hours and fifteen minute increments which results in a 24 hour day represented as 96 options.

Analogue clock face

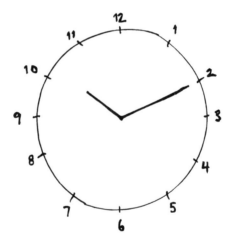

A different concept is the analogue clock that allows you to select the hour and then the minutes on a visual display. The user is forced to hunt for the correct hours and minutes - a pretty unnatural approach (such as dogs and cats living together in harmony) as analogue clocks have not been used for setting time since analogue alarm clocks went out of fashion.

Just an empty input field

```
9:00 AM
```

A empty input field lets the user type whatever they want, and they will. All the validation is up to the server and by this we mean you.

Tips

- Don't do empty input fields, they're a lot of work.

- Tell people what format you expect, 'hh:mm'

- Be very strict with what input you accept

- Limit the field length to the expected format. 'hh:mm' is 5 characters long.

Tests

- All of them!

Recurring events

Some events can happen more than once, like weddings. A recurring event might happen daily or be on a shorter or longer timescale. How do we get this information from users without falling back to a cron[6] like syntax? After all, you wouldn't want them to miss their weekly yoga class or morning walk.

...oh cron time... End of Line

Some points to consider

As with all things software development, it's best to find out what problem you're trying to solve first and then use that to design your user interface. Here are some questions to guide your investigation.

How often will the event repeat?

How often an event repeats is really based on one factor: how long between each event? To make it easier for people to understand, that factor can be split into two. One is the common time periods of day, week, month and year. The other is a multiplying factor, for example every 2 weeks; once a month, three times an hour.

---

[6]cron is the time-based job scheduler in Unix-like computer operating systems with a terse syntax

How many times will it repeat?

An open-ended event will never end. The event keeps occurring as it was specified, 3 times a day forever. Sometimes, we want our recurring events to stop, after 30 years we will have paid off our mortgage. In this case, we can say repeat this event 360 times (once a month) or repeat until January 9, 2043.

Do you need expressions like "The 2nd Wednesday of every month"?

Just because it can be done, doesn't mean it should. Recurring events become more complicated when we use terms like "the last Friday of each month", because the time between these events will differ. The aforementioned approach of just using a time period (months) and a factor (every 1) will no longer work.

Less common terms like "the 5th Friday of each month", are complicated in a different way. Not every month will have five Fridays.

Implementing these expressions is possible but labourious. You decide if it's necessary.

When does the event start?

While it isn't strictly related to recurrence, it is useful to consider a delayed start to events. I want my wedding anniversary reminder to be on September 9th, but I don't want it to start till next year.

Groundhog dates

It is possible to come unstuck in time and relive the same day over and over again. There's at least one way to deal with such a problem but unfortunately it's out of the scope of this book.

Recurring events

Some events can happen more than once, like weddings. A recurring event might happen daily or be on a shorter or longer timescale. How do we get this information from users without falling back to a cron[7] like syntax? After all, you wouldn't want them to miss their weekly yoga class or morning walk.

...oh cron time... End of Line

Some points to consider

As with all things software development, it's best to find out what problem you're trying to solve first and then use that to design your user interface. Here are some questions to guide your investigation.

How often will the event repeat?

How often an event repeats is really based on one factor: how long between each event? To make it easier for people to understand, that factor can be split into two. One is the common time periods of day, week, month and year. The other is a multiplying factor, for example every 2 weeks; once a month, three times an hour.

---

[7]cron is the time-based job scheduler in Unix-like computer operating systems with a terse syntax

How many times will it repeat?

An open-ended event will never end. The event keeps occurring as it was specified, 3 times a day forever. Sometimes, we want our recurring events to stop, after 30 years we will have paid off our mortgage. In this case, we can say repeat this event 360 times (once a month) or repeat until January 9, 2043.

Do you need expressions like "The 2nd Wednesday of every month"?

Just because it can be done, doesn't mean it should. Recurring events become more complicated when we use terms like "the last Friday of each month", because the time between these events will differ. The aforementioned approach of just using a time period (months) and a factor (every 1) will no longer work.

Less common terms like "the 5th Friday of each month", are complicated in a different way. Not every month will have five Fridays.

Implementing these expressions is possible but labourious. You decide if it's necessary.

When does the event start?

While it isn't strictly related to recurrence, it is useful to consider a delayed start to events. I want my wedding anniversary reminder to be on September 9th, but I don't want it to start till next year.

Groundhog dates

It is possible to come unstuck in time and relive the same day over and over again. There's at least one way to deal with such a problem but unfortunately it's out of the scope of this book.

Part IV

Under the hood

Test automation

Now that you have an overview it's time to dance —with the devil in the details. What follows is a look at some date and time mechanics. There are no pictures here, only diagrams.

In *Dealing With User Input*, we recommended using absolute dates as they're less likely to be misinterpreted. However now that you're under the hood, we recommend that you use relative dates in test automation. Unless you're also controlling the system time as part of that test. One day, that test date you assumed would always be in the future, will be in the past. If you try to counteract this by choosing a date far in the future, it's probably not relevant enough to make a good test. Absolute dates tend to result in 'golden' test data that have to be maintained as the test suite grows. Relative dates can be dynamically generated on the fly, reducing maintenance and the dependency on specific data.

Write your automated test code to use dates relative to the current date. Saying 'tomorrow' in a test, is both easy to understand and clearly shows it's in the future. As time progress, the relative dates will eventually get coverage over all date test cases, even ones you missed. If you do need to test what happens on certain dates, you can still use relative dates by introducing concepts like 'next leap year'.

Another avenue you can try is using relative dates one month in the future, so you have more time to fix things if your tests reveal you have problems on certain dates.

Converting time units

There are two problems with converting time units; most units are not divisible and some vary in length.

1 year = 26.08875 fortnights = 52.1775 weeks

1 month = 4.34812 weeks = 30.4368 days

1 month = 28, 29, 30 or 31 days

1 minute = 60 or 61 seconds

Variable Length Units

How do you convert a unit that varies in length e.g. a month into days?

You can work out the exact conversion for the current time e.g. how many days are in this month? But this approach is cumbersome because the value is contingent on the month.

For a general purpose approach, you can use an average or approximate length and deal with the inaccuracy. Some systems, for example, assume all months have 30 days.

Variable Significance Units

While two days might have the same duration in terms of hours, they might not be equal in terms of significance. If you're a business that is open Monday to Friday you shouldn't calculate the average visitors you get per day using a seven day week. The weekend is insignificant and should be excluded.

Most businesses experience seasonal effects. A ski resort for winter will have more customers and more employees. So a Monday in the summer isn't equal to a Monday in the winter.

Dealing with precision

As always, think about what you're using the number for. Using 4.4 week months is probably sufficient for working out the profit split on your banana stand[8]. But, if you work for Fat Cats International, embezzling millions of dollars, then the difference between 4.4 and 4.34812 weeks in a month really adds up.

Rolling over

This next bit might blow your mind! If we open a spreadsheet and add January 1, for any year into a cell, then add 7 days to that date and keep doing that until we get to the end of the year. The last date should be December 31 (if our year is not a leap year). Count how many dates we have. It should be 53. So, in conclusion, a year has 53 weeks, at 7 days each, a total of 371 days ...wait, what?

Ok, let's try using fortnights then, starting again on the 1st adding 14 days each time, it will take us 27 times to get to December 31 again. 27 fortnights at 14 days each is 378 days in the year. What?

One vanilla year has 365 days which is 52 weeks with a day left over. Because of this, the day of the week the year starts on occurs 53 times rather than 52. In a leap year, you will get two days that occur 53 times.

What has happened is that the first day of the week/fortnight, occurred 53 times but the rest of the week or fortnight happened in the next year. This is relevant if that day of the week is important. i.e. your payday.

---

[8]There's always money in the banana stand.

From years to fortnights?

You might be thinking that to convert a yearly figure to a fortnightly one all you have to do is divide by 26.

That works for most years, but if you're getting paid on a day that's happening 53 times this year you'll get paid 27 times.

On a long enough timeline you can average it out. If you multiply your yearly salary by 12 and then divide by 313 then you get your fortnightly pay. There are 313 fortnights over 12 years. You can divide this by two to get the weekly pay. The Australian Tax Office does it this way although it is still an approximation.

```
Fortnightly Salary = (Yearly Salary * 12) / 313
```

Getting to a second date

What date is one month from January 31?

Is it March 1 (30 days later), March 2 (31 days later), or February 28[9] (28 days later)?

The answer is February 28. The trick here is to remember you are adding a month and not adding days. You take the month part of the date and change it by the desired amount and you're done...mostly. Sometimes, you'll end up with an invalid date, like February 31. In this case, round down to the end of that month, February 28. Interestingly enough, you always round down regardless of whether you're adding or subtracting time. This isn't like normal addition, you don't carry over any remaining days. Thoth, the lunar god is always happy to take remaining days off your hands.

Give it a seconds thought

A common temptation when adding a period of time to a date is to represent the time as seconds and add it to the date. Using 3,600 seconds for an hour and 86,400 seconds for a day, on the surface makes tomorrow exactly 86,400 seconds away.

But that's wrong. Because of leap seconds, not all minutes are 60 seconds so your calculations will deteriorate from there. How many seconds do you use for varying quantities such as months that contain 28-31 days and years that have 365-366 days? Using seconds also doesn't

---

[9]It's not a leap year

account for daylight saving time where 3,600 seconds can be lost or gained in the blink of an eye.

When adding or subtracting dates the best thing to do is to break the date into its constitute parts.

`13/05/2013 @ 14:25:44` becomes:

```
day=13
month=5
year=2013
hour=14
minute=25
second=44
```

Now, if we want to add 1 day; then we increment the day value; so day becomes 14; and now we put it back together again.

`14/05/2013 @ 14:25:44`.

Or use a tested library[10].

Inclusive or exclusive date ranges

Consider a range of days, say March 1 until March 15. How many days are included?

If you count each day, it's 15. This is what's known as an inclusive date range. For an exclusive range, where you don't consider the first and last day, it's 13. If you include either the first or the last day but not both, it's 14. Remember to tell people what type of range you're expecting.

Why does this matter? Let's explore writing a query that gets data for our inclusive 15 day range. Before we start, whenever we show a date with no time component e.g. 15-Mar-2012, our system will conveniently evaluate it as 15-Mar-2012 00:00:00. Your mileage may vary.

---

[10]Ssh... secret! This is the correct answer

Code!

First up, some SQL that looks correct to the casual observer but...

```
SELECT * FROM some_table WHERE date_created >= '01-Mar-2012'
    AND date_created <= '15-Mar-2012';
```

Your query has now included all the records from the first second of March 1 and the first second of March 15... and ignores the rest of the day. That's 86,399 seconds![11]

```
February 28 @ 23:59 - excluded ✔

March  1 @ 00:00 - included ✔
March  1 @ 00:01 - included ✔
March 15 @ 00:00 - included ✔

March 15 @ 00:01 - excluded ✗
March 15 @ 23:59 - excluded ✗
March 15 @ 23:60 - excluded ✗

March 16 @ 00:00 - excluded  ✔
```

Lets fix this and add 1 day

```
SELECT * FROM some_table WHERE date_created >= '01-Mar-2012'
    AND date_created <= '16-Mar-2012'
```

Better, but still subtly wrong as you are also including all the records you want and any created on the first second on March 16. This is because the equal sign includes March 16 at 00:00:00s.

```
February 28 @ 23:59 - excluded ✔

March  1 @ 00:00 - included ✔
March  1 @ 00:01 - included ✔
March 15 @ 00:00 - included ✔
March 15 @ 00:01 - included ✔
March 15 @ 23:59 - included ✔
March 15 @ 23:60 - included ✔

March 16 @ 00:00 - included  ✗
```

---

[11]or 86,400 in a day with a leap second

Switching it about again

```
SELECT * FROM some_table WHERE date_created >  '01-Mar-2012'
    AND date_created <= '15-Mar-2012'
```

This is also wrong as we are missing all records created during the first second of the day.

```
February 28 @ 23:59 - excluded  ✔

March 1 @ 00:00 - excluded  ✗

March 1 @ 00:01 - included  ✔
March 15 @ 00:00 - included  ✔
March 15 @ 00:01 - included  ✔
March 15 @ 23:59 - included  ✔
March 15 @ 23:60 - included  ✔

March 16 @ 00:00 - excluded  ✔
```

Being more precise can result in less frequent bugs

```
SELECT * FROM some_table WHERE date_created >= '01-Mar-2012
    00:00:00' AND date_created <= '15-Mar-2012 23:59:59'
```

This query only fails when we have a leap second and that pesky record created at 23:59:60 doesn't return.

```
February 28 @ 23:59 - excluded  ✔

March 1 @ 00:00 - included  ✔
March 1 @ 00:01 - included  ✔
March 15 @ 00:00 - included  ✔
March 15 @ 00:01 - included  ✔
March 15 @ 23:59 - included  ✔

March 15 @ 23:60 - excluded  ✗

March 16 @ 00:00 - excluded  ✔
```

The correct query

```
SELECT * FROM some_table WHERE date_created >= '01-Mar-2012'
    AND date_created < '16-Mar-2012'
```

This includes all of the seconds from the first day right through to the last second of the 15th and any potential leap seconds.

```
February 28 @ 23:59 - excluded  ✔

March 1  @ 00:00 - included  ✔
March 1  @ 00:01 - included  ✔
March 15 @ 00:00 - included  ✔
March 15 @ 00:01 - included  ✔
March 15 @ 23:59 - included  ✔
March 15 @ 23:60 - included  ✔

March 16 @ 00:00 - excluded  ✔
```

Tests

So what are some test cases when dealing with a range of dates:

- February 28 @ 23:59 (1 second before; should be excluded)

- March 1 @ 00:00 (first second)

- March 15 @ 23:59 (last second of last day)

- March 15 @ 23:60 (last leap second of last day)

- March 16 @ 00:00 (1 second after; should be excluded)

- Don't forget leap years when doing a second after or before.

- Try out year boundaries for your start and end dates.

What if multiple date constructs are used?

Let's say you're storing a date in a database using a type that includes both the date and time component and the class you are using in your object persistence layer represents only the 'Date'. In such a case, it's likely that the database will use 00:00:00 to represent the time component for each date that it is given. When you examine your date object, it will look fine, because it knows to ignore the time component.

What happens when you need to tune up performance and bypass your persistence layer? You're no longer getting the nice mapping that it was giving you. It's now really easy to accidentally specify a date range incorrectly because you're mentally thinking about each date as not having a time component.

Example

Let's begin with a record in the database represented in two ways:

```
database record: 15 May, 2012 00:00:00
object.to_string: 15 May, 2012
```

In your code, you might have the following statement:

```
if date == Date.today then
  do_awesome_magic_thing(date)
end
```

Now, does Date.today resolve to any record that has a time component of 00:00:00 or one that is the range of 00:00:00 -> 23:59:59? This is important to know.

Let's say you drop down into SQL to improve the insert performance. In doing this, you use something like sysdate[12] to store in the date field. This adds the time part but you didn't pay attention to that.

```
database record: 15 May, 2012 12:23:46
object.to_string: 15 May, 2012
```

Now, this will still work as the object persistence layer handles the conversion for you. Six months later you decide to replace the if-statement with SQL as well; it just wasn't performing well enough!

```
SELECT * FROM some_table WHERE date = Date.today
```

However, this will now fail as a date = Date.today only works if the time part is 00:00:00. Because of our poor use of sysdate, and failing to understand what our data was before we wrote the code we now have a bug.

---

[12]It gives you the current date/time on one database

ℹ️ Time !== Time

A friend sent me a problem he was having with some SQL statements on SQL Server. When doing a comparison less than or equal to a date with 6 zeroes in the decimal place it returned zero results. When specifying a 7th zero it returned a result. Looking at the results below you can see the three queries he ran.

```
select * from org where id = 105 AND date <=
    '2007−05−15 12:00:00 ';
(no results)

select * from org where id = 105 AND date <=
    '2007−05−15 12:00:00.000000 ';
(no results)

select * from org where id = 105 AND date <=
    '2007−05−15 12:00:00.0000000 ';

(1 result)
| My Company Ltd | 2007−05−15 12:00:00.000000+0800 |
```

There was something strange about how that date was being stored or it could have been an artefact of a decimal rounding. The moral of the story is that you can't just assume time will work for you in your application. You need to understand the type of data you have, you need to know where it comes from, you need to isolate time from your system, and finally, you need to write tests.

Understanding the limits of time

How you represent dates in your program can be the cause of bugs that occur at some future point. You could literally run out time. You might have decided to count seconds using a 32-bit unsigned integer (a non-negative number with a maximum of 2 to the power of 32). Such a method will give you 136 years before you run out of space. If you use a signed integer (a number between -2^{31} to $+2^{31}$) then you'll only get 68 years, which is how long the unix epoch is. It counts the seconds since 1970 and runs out in 2038.

If you chose to count years using a 2 digit number you get 100 years before you run out. However, if you skip the years before you invented computers then you run out pretty quickly.

In some cases you just need to accept your design decision. Write it down so that future generations know why you made this decision and move on. This is perfectly acceptable, the future version of you will be far better equipped to solve the problems anyway.

In other cases, if you can't live with such a setup, you need to use a different tool or a different library. Don't make your work harder by trying to use a tool not designed for this work. You don't use a hand plane to cut down a tree because you don't have a chainsaw at hand. Go buy a chainsaw.

Optionality

It's possible for a date or part of a date to be optional. You may ask for a date of birth but not care about whether or not you get that information. Perhaps only some of the information is known. There are plenty of people in the world who don't know their own birth year let alone birth date.

In these cases it's best if you write your own custom date structure, or wrap an existing one. A simple approach is to store each date time component as a separate, optional field.

Even for complete dates, we've seen experienced developers use a date-time with the date set to 1/1/1 when they just wanted a time and we've seen systems where a null date is stored as 1/1/1900.

Whether intentional or unintentional how do you factor such behaviour into your algorithms? Are you looking for absent dates when they are stored as valid dates? Do you show the date 'January 1, 1900', on the UI when it shouldn't be displayed at all.

This approach will make your code harder to maintain and is often a failing of your domain model. If you use a time when you need a time, a date when you need a date, then you're going to have fewer problems.

Sorting dates

How easy it is to sort dates depends on the programming language, available libraries and how the dates are stored. In modern environments, you can simply use a sort function.

If you're dealing with dates represented as strings, like in a file name, things get tricky. Usually, it's simpler to convert the strings to a proper date object and to sort them, than it is to mess around with all the rules required to sort dates represented as a string. If you're stuck with strings, your best bet is the largest to smallest 'yyyy-mm-dd' format so you can sort them as if they were numbers.

The ISO 8601 standard date format[21]. It's in lexicographical order

(ASCIIbetical) of the representations equivalent to the chronological order of the dates.

```
2010-05-01
2010-05-02
2010-06-01
```

If you didn't write them this way you would end up with a list like this:

```
1-05-2010
1-06-2010  ✗ Out of place
2-05-2010
```

As you can see, June 1 is out of place because the computer treated it like a number when sorting. You also need to ensure that each of your date parts have padded zeroes to a fixed width otherwise you will end up with:

```
2010-05-1
2010-05-10  ✗ Out of place
2010-05-2
```

If you want any other format (dd-mm-yyyy), you end up having to parse the string and understand the date. If you want to include the hours, minutes or seconds in your date, then you need to use 24 hour time.

```
2010-05-01  10:43:12
2010-05-01  17:43:12
2010-05-01  22:43:12
```

Because the am/pm part is at the end of the string and will end up with this:

```
2010-05-01  05:43:12 pm  ✗ Out of place
2010-05-01  10:43:12 am
2010-05-01  10:43:12 pm
```

Tips

- Write the date from largest period to smallest

- Make all time periods a fixed length, pad with zeroes

- Use 24 hour time

Tests

The best way to test sorting of dates is to make sure you have one of each of the following dates and see what comes out!

- May 1

- May 2

- May 10

- June 1

- July 1, at 10 in the morning

- July 1, at 9 in the evening

- Two dates on August 1, at 8 a.m, in multiple time zones

- May 1, in a later year

If you get something wrong then any one of the following will occur:

- The June 1 date will appear in between the May dates if not sorted correctly.

- May 10 will sort before the May 2 if you use alphabetic sorting

- The 9 pm date will sort before the 10 am date when using 12-hour time

- If the time zone is not being considered, then the sorting will be incorrect for the August dates

- The dates from later years should be sorted at the end

Part V

Reality bytes

What follows are real world examples of the places we've been and the situations we've ended up in that inspired us to write this book. They've taught us that it doesn't usually take much to make a system easy to test —just a willingness to experiment and to isolate your system from time.

A Bank

This bank, like most banks we've worked at, had a mainframe at its core. Mainframes are expensive, which makes having multiple environments eye-wateringly costly. Mainframes are often embedded in 20 years of IT cement, making them next to impossible to replace. Because of these factors there was one development mainframe shared across the whole company, you couldn't go changing time on it all willy-nilly.

But, being a bank, they needed to be able to test time-related things faster than real time. Their solution was to run time at twice normal speed on the mainframe. This meant you could test a mortgage in 12.5 years rather than 25. It was common for tests to take over a year to run. Because this was a shared resource, it also meant anyone could come along and change the data out from under you; so you would have to start all over again. It took so much time that some tests would have to be handed down through several generations of testers.

The bank handled this problem by marking the test data clearly with threats, so no one dared touch it.

How did we work in these conditions? To remain sane, we abstracted the system clock from the code by creating a method in the application that returned the time. Mostly, it would return the system time but when testing, it would return times of our choosing. We then had to go spelunking to find all the batch jobs that happened under the hood. They needed rework so they could run individual bits of data on demand, rather than running all the data at certain times. This endeavour was costly and time consuming, but in the end it allowed us to use automated testing and have a build that could be measured in minutes rather than years.

A Taxation Office

A taxation system, like any system built on the whims of politicians, will have different rules for different years. This is further complicated by the fact that any individual or business can submit revisions to their tax return years after the original lodgement.

The goal of working on a system like this is to decouple the year the tax return is for from the year it was lodged. For example, if I revise my 2012 lodgement in 2013 or 2014 it should behave in the same way as if it was lodged 2012.

In the real world, it normally doesn't make sense to lodge a tax return in the future. But it's damn handy for testing. This allowed us to test our changes before they became available in production. It also allowed us to establish history for multi-year calculations.

An Internet Company

This company had a system in which it was easy to move time forward and impossible to move it backward. Each environment was initialized with today's date and skipped forward a month whenever someone wanted to test a monthly batch job. Whenever their servers hit 2038, they would lose a few days rebuilding the environment, before starting again.

When we got there, we explored the system, and it turned out that it was possible to backdate the creation of records. It was also possible to configure the system so the monthly job could be run every day for a different subset of records. When we created a new backdated record, we could specify which monthly job subset it belonged to. We would then run that and did not need to move time forward at any point.

An Advertising Company

The company had a system that was responsible for capturing and reporting all the user events across the advertising network. The events would come in, be sliced and diced, and then stored in a data warehouse.

Eventually it appeared on a report that contained up to one year's history.

There were two aspects of this system that made testing hard. Firstly, to prevent people from sending in old data or changing numbers on reports already generated, they blocked any event older than one month. This made setting up historical testing data impossible.

We changed the system to make the acceptable event age configurable. Internally, we allowed events up to 18 months old. This allowed us to build history for testing reports with over a year's worth of data.

Secondly, because of the tens of millions of events coming in each day, the database was partitioned daily to keep it performing. Originally, we were told it was too hard to auto-generate the partitions for 12 months of history. We had a go anyway and it turned out it wasn't; so we threw together a ruby script to generate the necessary SQL.

Thanks

Congratulations! You now know everything we know about dates and times. We thank you for your time. We wrote this book, so you would have a single point of reference on dates and times. You don't need to hold all of this in your head, just remember this book and refer to it as needed. We suggest buying a second copy as an offline backup.

Mike Bain, Ryan Boucher and Ash Rollke

Bibliography

[1] Wikipedia Contributors, *Sunday* Wikipedia, The Free Encyclopedia. 2013. http://bit.ly/WikiSunday (Accessed March 21, 2013)

[2] Wikipedia Contributors, *Egyptian Calendar* Wikipedia, The Free Encyclopedia. 2013. http://bit.ly/EgyptianCalendar (Accessed March 17, 2013)

[3] Wikipedia Contributors, *Thoth* Wikipedia, The Free Encyclopedia. 2013. http://bit.ly/WikiThoth (Accessed March 17, 2013)

[4] Wikipedia Contributors, *Planck Time* Wikipedia, The Free Encyclopedia. 2013. http://bit.ly/PlanckTime (Accessed March 19, 2013)

[5] Wikipedia Contributors, *Railway Time* Wikipedia, The Free Encyclopedia. 2013. http://bit.ly/RailwayTime (Accessed March 19, 2013)

[6] Martin Fowler, *Time Point* martingfowler.com 2000. http://bit.ly/TimePoint (Accessed March 19, 2013)

[7] Wikipedia Contributors, *UTC+08:45* Wikipedia, The Free Encyclopedia. 2012. http://bit.ly/UTC845 (Accessed January 9, 2013)

[8] Wikipedia Contributors, *Time In Australia* Wikipedia, The Free Encyclopedia. 2013. http://bit.ly/TimeInAustralia (Accessed March 19, 2013)

[9] C. G. P. Grey *Daylight Saving Time Explained* cgpgrey.com 2013. http://bit.ly/DaylightSavingTimeExplained (Accessed March 19, 2013)

[10] Charles Q. Choi *Does Daylight Saving Time Conserve Energy?* Scientific American, a Division of Nature America, Inc. 2009. http://www.scientificamerican.com/article.cfm?id=does-daylight-saving-times-save-energy (Accessed January 9, 2013)

[11] Wikipedia Contributors, *Universal Time* Wikipedia, The Free Encyclopedia. 2013. http://bit.ly/WikiUniversalTime (Accessed January 9, 2013)

[12] Cade Metz *'Leap Second' Bug Wreaks Havoc Across Web* Wired.com 2012 http://www.wired.com/wiredenterprise/2012/07/leap-second-bug-wreaks-havoc-with-java-linux/ (Accessed January 9, 2013)

[13] Robert McMillan & Cade Metz *The Inside Story of the Extra Second That Crashed the Web* Wired.com 2012. http://www.wired.com/wiredenterprise/2012/07/leap-second-glitch-explained/ (Accessed January 9, 2013)

[14] Robert M. Candey *Requirements for handling leap seconds in CDF* NASA Goddard Space Flight Center, Code 672, Greenbelt MD 20771 USA 2011. http://bit.ly/nasagps (Accessed March 19, 2013)

[15] Christopher Pascoe *Time, technology and leaping seconds* Google Inc. 2011. http://bit.ly/leapsmear (Accessed March 19, 2013)

[16] Zachary Yontz *The Easter Bunny Phenomenon* 26 April 2007

[17] Wikipedia Contributors, *Workweek and Weekend* Wikipedia, The Free Encyclopedia. 2013. http://bit.ly/WorkweekAndWeekend (Accessed March 19, 2013)

[18] Wikipedia Contributors, *Workweek and Weekend* Wikipedia, The Free Encyclopedia. 2013. http://bit.ly/AusPublicHoliday (Accessed March 19, 2013)

[19] Wikipedia Contributors, *Julian Day Number* Wikipedia, The Free Encyclopedia. 2013. http://bit.ly/JulianDayNumber (Accessed April 5, 2013)

[20] Oracle *Testing Your Price List* Oracle 2012. http://bit.ly/OracleBS (Accessed March 21, 2013)

94

[21] Wikipedia Contributors, *ISO 8601* Wikipedia, The Free Encyclopedia. 2013. http://bit.ly/WikiISO8601 (Accessed March 19,
2013)

Further Reading

[1] *IANA Time Zones* www.iana.org/time-zones

[2] *Wikipedia - Seriation (archaeology)* http://en.wikipedia.org/
wiki/Seriation_(archaeology)

[3] *Wikipedia - Time Zone* http://en.wikipedia.org/wiki/Time_
zone

[4] *Wikipedia - Resolution* http://en.wiktionary.org/wiki/
resolution

[5] *Wikipedia - Leap Second* http://en.wikipedia.org/wiki/Leap_
second

[6] *Wikipedia - Date Format By Country* http://en.wikipedia.org/
wiki/Date_format_by_country

[7] *Wikipedia - Civil Time* http://en.wikipedia.org/wiki/Civil_
time

[8] *Wikipedia - Buffalo buffalo Buffalo buffalo buffalo buffalo Buffalo buffalo* http://en.wikipedia.org/wiki/
BuffaloBuffaloBuffaloBuffalo

[9] *jquery.timepickr* http://haineault.com/media/jquery/
ui-timepickr/page/

[10] *Living on Zionist Time* http://darwinawards.com/darwin/
darwin1999-38.html

[11] *More falsehoods programmers believe about time; "wisdom of the crowd" edition* http://infiniteundo.com/post/25509354022/more-falsehoods-programmers-believe-about-time-wisdom

[12] *Falsehoods Programmers Believe* http://www.metafilter.com/117073/Falsehoods-Programmers-Believe#4405410

[13] *Computer-Related Risks* http://www.csl.sri.com/users/neumann/cal.html

[14] *The CHECKS Pattern Language of Information Integrity* http://c2.com/ppr/checks.html#4

[15] *Time Scales* http://www.ucolick.org/~sla/leapsecs/timescales.html

www.ingramcontent.com/pod-product-compliance
Lightning Source LLC
Chambersburg PA
CBHW052148070326

40689CB00050B/2515